MORE BIRDS OF THE DAY

Plate 1.—The hobby—most graceful of British falcons.

MORE BIRDS OF THE DAY

By

ERIC J. HOSKING

F.R.P.S., M.B.O.U.

AND

CYRIL W. NEWBERRY

B.Sc., A.M.I.Mech.E., F.R.P.S.

Collins

FOURTEEN ST. JAMES'S PLACE, LONDON

1946

By the same Authors

INTIMATE SKETCHES FROM BIRD LIFE (*Country Life, 1940*)

THE ART OF BIRD PHOTOGRAPHY (*Country Life, 1944*)

BIRDS OF THE DAY (*Collins, 1944*)

BIRDS OF THE NIGHT (*Collins, 1945*)

THE SWALLOW (*Collins, 1946*)

PRINTED IN GREAT BRITAIN BY
JAMES COND LTD., FOR THE PUBLISHERS
BLOCKS BY THE SUN ENGRAVING CO., LTD.
1946

To the memory of

JIM VINCENT

Contents

Preface

When we set out to prepare our earlier volume, *Birds of the Day*, we did so in answer to numerous requests for a book containing some of our best photographs. We set out to produce a book for the reader's enjoyment, and our publishers played their part handsomely, but even so we were astonished and overwhelmed by the reception the book received. It has far exceeded all our expectations. That is our justification for producing this further volume.

More Birds of the Day is planned on similar lines to its forerunner. As before, the contents comprise a miscellaneous collection of birds; some extremely local and rare, and others known and loved by everyone throughout the land. Again, our subjects follow no rigid plan, but have been arranged to give interest and variety. It matters little whether we are watching the robin in the intimacy of our garden or the Slavonian grebe in the remote seclusion of a Scottish loch. There is a fascination in both of them, as in all birds, and we shall be happy if, through the medium of this book, we can pass on to our readers some of the pleasure we ourselves have derived from our experiences in the field.

We have tried to make our text as accurate as possible and to that end have asked Dr. Stuart Smith to read through our manuscript. This he has gladly done, and we thank him for several helpful suggestions he has made.

As may well be imagined, the pictures reproduced in this volume represent the results of many years' work, and in obtaining them we have been greatly helped by many people. Among them we would mention in particular the numerous friends who from time to time have advised us of interesting occurrences, and the land-owners and their agents who have granted us the facilities indispensable to bird photography. Neither do we forget the many kindnesses we have been shown at the hands of the workers on the various estates, ranging from hospitality to assistance with the hundred-and-one odd tasks that go to make up the bird photographer's day. One of the things that has impressed us as we have gone about the country in search of birds has been the courtesy and helpfulness to be met with at every turn, and as we cast our minds back we think with pleasure of the very many friends we have made in the course of bird watching.

ERIC HOSKING.
CYRIL NEWBERRY.

February, 1946.

The Hobby

THE HOBBY may be likened in some respects to its better-known cousin, the peregrine falcon, but whereas the latter is a resident in the British Isles and may occur in most parts where suitable cliffs or rocky crags provide it with nesting sites, the hobby is only a summer visitor and is confined chiefly to that part of England lying south of the river Thames and to a few counties in the South Midlands.

Wooded heathland, where the trees occur in small clumps, is the favourite haunt of the hobby; and it shows a particular liking for pine trees. Like the other falcons, the hobby does not build a nest of its own, but relies on finding the disused nest of some other species. That of the carrion crow is the most frequently used, but old nests of rooks, magpies, jays and sparrow-hawks also serve on occasions.

The hobby is very late to begin nesting, and although the birds arrive in this country in the second half of April and soon settle in the districts where they will nest, it is usually June before the hen begins to lay her eggs, and July before the chicks are hatched.

The nest we had under observation in 1945, and which we illustrate in these pages, was about twenty-seven feet high in a Scots pine on a Surrey heath. It was found by Messrs. Anthony Wootton and Hugh Clutton-Brock, who hurriedly advised us of its location and helped in our preparations for photography. We were also assisted by, and acknowledge our gratitude to, Field-Marshal Lord Alanbrooke, who, in addition to his better-known achievements, is a keen ornithologist; and we were delighted to find that, in spite of the pressure of work that inevitably falls on the Chief of the Imperial General Staff at the close of a major war, he was able, during a short leave on his return from the Potsdam Conference, to spend a few hours in the hide and to make a colour ciné film of the hobby.

Both birds of the pair were in fine plumage, their slate-blue wings and backs having a fine sheen and not a feather out of place. It was thrilling to see them at close quarters. The head is finely proportioned and of striking appearance, both on account of the way the dark crown and moustachial streaks contrast with the whitish chin and cheeks, and because of the large, dark and piercing eyes; and the hooked bill is particularly neat in its smallness; but the head does not attract all the attention, for the breast is beautifully flecked with dark brownish markings on a cream background, and below that is a splash of colour in the reddish-orange thighs and the yellow legs.

The young hobbies, like the merlins we included in *Birds of the Day*, were covered at first in plentiful white down, which gradually gave way to brownish feathers on the back and to creamy ones on the underparts. In common with all young predators, they had insatiable appetites, and the parents were kept very busy supplying their needs. Both adults engaged in hunting, but by far the larger share was done by the cock, particularly while the chicks were small. Sometimes he would pass the food to the hen in flight as we shall presently describe, but sometimes he alighted in a favourite tree a little distance from the nest and thence called the hen to him. He waited for her to perch beside him, and then, it seemed, though we were unable to see this with certainty, the two birds indulged in a little fondling before the hen came back with the prey. She would bring it to the nest, carrying it in her talons and passing it up to her bill just prior to alighting. Having settled on the back of the nest, she put down the prey, gripped it under one foot and, seizing a piece of it in her bill, she pulled up and tore it off with a twist of her head. It was interesting to notice that, when small birds were brought as food, they were nearly always decapitated and usually well plucked, and we were often, in consequence, unable to identify the prey. We saw it, however, to consist chiefly of small passerines, and were able to distinguish a blackbird, a blue-tit and a sky-lark. We saw no moths, dragon-flies, beetles or other insects brought to this nest, but they are reported by other observers as forming part of the diet of the hobby.

Fascinating as the hobby is at the nest, it is as a master of flight that the bird merits particular study. It seems to revel in its remarkable powers, and, especially in the period just before nesting begins, it may be seen disporting itself high in the sky; twisting, circling and diving, and making all manner of aerial evolutions as if for the sheer joy of doing so. It can dive on and capture the swallow and is said to outfly the swift, but with all its speed it has wonderful powers of manœuvre which make its performance so enchanting. Undoubtedly, however, the high-light of the display is the food-pass when the hen meets the cock to take from him the proceeds of the chase.

One evening, while watching from the hide, we heard the cock calling in the distance, "kew, kew, kew," and immediately the hen flew out from the nest to meet him. We saw her apparently chasing him at great speed to the accompaniment of a duet of rapid calls. She quickly caught up with him and the two birds flew towards each other on rapidly converging paths. They seemed to collide at lightning speed, but, as they did so, they each rolled outwards, swung up their tarsi, and the hen snatched the prey from her mate's talons. The two birds parted as quickly as they had come together, and the hen returned to the nest.

Three times in the course of our observations we saw such passes, and we know that others took place outside our field of vision. Words fail to convey adequately the fascination of this remarkable spectacle. It is performed at such speed that nothing, it seems, can save the birds from a disastrous collision. In fact, had we not known what to expect we should have assumed the birds were fighting viciously, the one to drive the other away from its territory.

Plate 2.—The young hobbies were covered in plentiful white down.

Plate 3.—The hobby feeds her chicks.

Plate 4.—The young hobbies begin to show their feathers.

The Woodpeckers

By a process of evolution, all living creatures adopt particular modes of life and, at the same time, develop certain characteristics to fit them for those conditions. The large eyes of the nocturnal birds are perhaps the most familiar example of this process, but there are many other striking illustrations. One of the most remarkable among the diurnal birds is the family of woodpeckers. They are essentially arboreal birds, nesting and spending the greater part of their time in the trees, and it is interesting to see how they have developed to suit their environment.

All of them—there are three which nest regularly in the British Isles—excavate their own nesting-holes, and for this particular purpose they have remarkably strong, chisel-like bills; but strength of bill alone would not ensure the power to dig a hole in a tree; the bird must have the means of applying itself to the job. This is provided by large, powerful claws which, arranged two pointing forwards and two backwards, enable the bird to obtain a firm grip on the bark of the tree; and by the short, stiff tail, which, pressed against the trunk as shown in our illustrations, serves not merely to support the bird, but also to take the reaction from the blow of the bill during the digging operations.

The largest and best-known of our British woodpeckers is the green. It is not uncommon in the woods and wooded parklands of England and Wales, but its numbers fall off as we approach the Scottish Border, and it is quite rare in Scotland, appearing only as an occasional wanderer. Ireland, too, seems to be outside its range, and only a very few have been reported from there.

We most often become aware of the presence of a green woodpecker by hearing its laughing call come ringing across the fields. Indeed, so notable is this that country people often call the bird the "yaffle." It is a note that is difficult to describe, yet, once heard, is not easily mistaken or forgotten; and, because it carries well, we hear it far more often than we see its originator. As the bird comes into view our first impression is of a fairly fast, yet laboured, undulating flight; the bird appearing to rest and glide momentarily after every few wing beats: but closer acquaintance reveals the green woodpecker as a sturdy bird with considerable power in its wings. It alights on a tree, and we immediately see that here it is truly at home. It ascends the trunk in a series of hops, using its strong bill to break off small pieces of bark here and there to discover lurking insects, and, as we watch from the intimacy of a hide, we are able to see the peculiarly well-developed tongue at work. It is unusually long, and flashes rapidly in and out, probing deep into crevices in search of the larvæ of wood-boring insects. The point is hard and barbed and this, no doubt, facilitates the capture of the woodpecker's prey. At this point we should perhaps mention

[*Continued on page* 18.

Plate 5.—The green woodpecker and young at nesting hole.

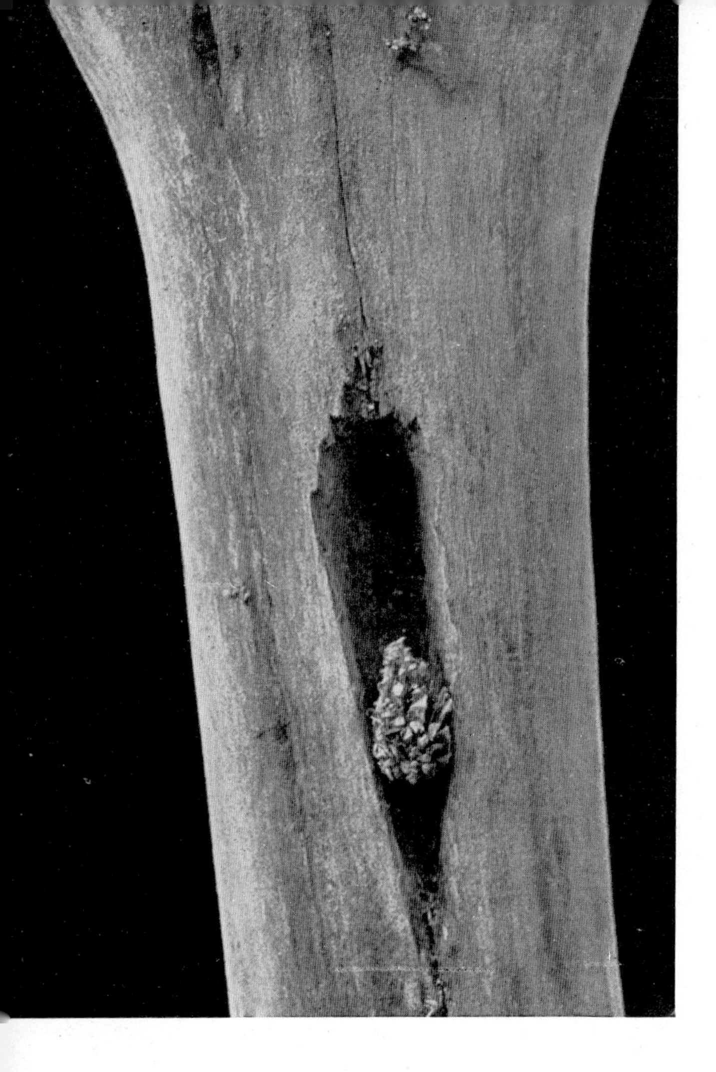

Plate 6.—Tapered hole made by great spotted woodpecker for holding pine cones.

Plate 7.—Great spotted woodpecker found dead with an oak gall impaled on its bill.

Plate 8.—Great spotted woodpecker with food.

that much of the green woodpecker's food is collected on the ground, and the bird shows a particular liking for ants and their larvæ. We notice, too, from our vantage point, the handsome yellowish-green plumage and the blood-red crown, and we reflect on how much beauty is missed by the casual observer watching his birds from a distance.

The great spotted woodpecker is found in much the same places as the green, and in addition it breeds in some parts of Southern and Central Scotland, but it is less often seen because of its more retiring disposition. Like its larger cousin, the great spotted woodpecker advertises its presence in the breeding season by its call, the loud resonant "drumming" as the bird rapidly taps with its bill on to a dead branch being a sound quite distinct from any other. Its boldly marked black and white plumage, seen in conjunction with its tree-climbing habits, makes it unlikely to be confused with any other bird except perhaps the lesser spotted woodpecker; and as this latter bird is much smaller, being little larger than a sparrow, identification should not be difficult.

In addition to larvæ and insects, the great spotted woodpecker not infrequently attacks pine cones, and it holds these for breaking open by wedging them in a crevice of bark or in a specially excavated tapered hole, as we show in the photograph on page 16. Quite large cones are broken with ease, but the power of the bill is not always to the bird's advantage, and we were recently shown a great spotted woodpecker that had driven its bill so firmly into an oak gall that it had been unable to extricate itself and had starved to death.

The smallest of the family, the lesser spotted woodpecker, is the least frequently seen. It is even more retiring, as a rule, than the others, and spends most of its time high up in woodland trees, but as we have seen with other species, exceptional pairs sometimes occur, and we were fortunate enough to photograph one pair of lesser spotted woodpeckers that nested in a greengage tree only forty inches above the ground and within fifteen yards of a woodman's cottage.

Plate 9.—Lesser spotted woodpecker with grubs of wood-boring beetle.

The Wryneck

CLOSELY ALLIED to the woodpeckers, yet differing from them in many respects, is the wryneck. This bird is comparatively little known, and justly so, for it is extraordinarily secretive as well as being extremely local in its occurrence.

The wryneck is a summer visitor, reaching our shores during the early part of April, but though some birds pass northwards along our eastern seaboard on their way to Scandinavia, there is not much general spread across the country and the comparatively few birds that breed here tend to stay in the south-east. There is evidence that the range of the bird has decreased compared with former times, and that in many places where it used to breed it is now a rare vagrant; and, moreover, the wryneck has decreased considerably in numbers during recent years, though from what cause we are unable to say.

Unlike its cousins, the woodpeckers, the wryneck does not excavate its own nesting-hole, but likes to use a natural hole in either a tree, a bank, or a wall, or it will sometimes use a nesting-box. As will be seen from the illustrations, the bird lacks the strong bill of the woodpeckers, and neither has it such a short stiff tail. With its strong claws it does, however, cling quite firmly to rough vertical surfaces, and is quite at home climbing the trunks of trees; but it is more frequently to be seen perching across the upper branches.

Because of its shy habits, the wryneck is often first noticed by its call. A shrill "quee-quee-quee-quee" attracts our attention, and on looking up we see a greyish-brown bird making a short, undulating flight from one tree to another. It alights probably high up and almost obscured from our view, but we notice how remarkably the bird's plumage matches its background of trees, and we realise how difficult it would be to spot the bird if we had not first seen it move.

Although the wryneck is so largely arboreal, like the green woodpecker it obtains a large part of its food on the ground, and seems particularly fond of ants and their pupæ. At the nest we illustrate, it was amazing to watch the birds come back after feeding. Their bills were crammed with a mixture of black ants and white "eggs," and there was considerable leakage in the process of tranferring the food to the chicks in the hole. Soon after the parents had left, there came a regular stream of ants, rushing out of the hole and trying to make good their escape. While the chicks were small, many of the ants did manage to get away, but when the young wrynecks were old enough to come to the mouth of the hole they caught many of these escaping ants by flashing out their long tongues. The tongue must be sticky at the tip, for the birds had no difficulty in collecting the insects from the cracks and crannies of the oak bark.

By the time they left the nest the young wrynecks closely resembled their

[*Continued on page* 23.

Plate 10.—The wryneck.

Plates 11 and 12.—The wryneck brings food to the nest.

Plate 13.—The young wryneck is very like its parents.

parents, except that they had plain cream breasts and rather shorter bills. Fortuitously, we had a good view of one of them which alighted on a branch only a foot or so below the nest of a spotted flycatcher that we had under observation. We noticed that, in the course of feeding, the tongue flashed out and curved round the branch, poking into crevices that the bird could not see; suggesting that food is collected by a sense of touch, as well as, or rather than, by sight.

The Goldcrest

THIS TIT-LIKE little creature is the smallest bird to be found in the British Isles. Only three and a half inches long, and weighing but a fraction of an ounce, it is, nevertheless, extremely active and vivacious, and we are constantly amazed at its apparently inexhaustible energy.

The goldcrest is predominantly a bird of the coniferous woodlands, having a marked preference for spruce; but particularly in the winter, when our birds are reinforced by large numbers from the Continent, the goldcrest is also to be found in mixed woods and copses. At such a time the birds move about in flocks, often in company with other tits; but with the approach of the breeding season, the flocks break up, the visitors go home, and the goldcrest becomes comparatively inconspicuous again in his woodland haunts.

It is by his call-note that the goldcrest usually makes his presence known. A very thin, high-pitched "see-see-see" somewhere above us as we walk through the woods is our first clue, and then, looking up, we see a diminutive form flitting about from branch to branch. It hangs here and there from a spray, twisting itself with great agility as it examines the foliage for spiders and other insects, and then quickly moves on to another perch. It seems to have no regard for our presence and continues the hunt without interruption.

The plumage of the goldcrest is by no means striking, though when seen at close quarters the crest is brilliant enough, being a bright yellow colour at the front and shading to a reddish-orange at the back. The crest can be raised and spread to a considerable extent, and is used thus in the courtship display. The male perches facing his mate, and bowing slightly, with wings partially spread and drooped, he quivers the feathers of the crest, and raises them again and again to present a fiery patch of colour in front of her. The crest is set off by a black border, but for the rest of its plumage the goldcrest is a dull greenish-brown on the upper part, with small whitish bars on the wings, and the underside is a light buff.

The goldcrest is fairly generally distributed in the British Isles except for the islands off the North and North-West of Scotland, but it seems that its existence is somewhat precarious. In the hard winter of 1916-17 the species was practically exterminated, and took some years to recover; and it suffered again in the winters of 1939-40-41; but the bird seems to have remarkable powers of recuperation, and we are glad to find it regaining its numerical strength.

Plate 14.—The goldcrest—smallest bird in the British Isles.

Plate 15.—The rooks gather in a tree near the rookery.

The Rook

In a general way the rook can be regarded as a well-known bird. It occurs in all parts of the British Isles where trees provide it with nesting-sites; and because of its comparatively large size and the fact that it is essentially gregarious at all seasons, it is a conspicuous feature of our native avifauna. The clusters of tree-top nests that comprise a rookery are prominent in many landscapes. Some of these rookeries have been occupied for centuries, for the rook is a bird of rather fixed habits and returns season after season to the same site, if not to the same nest. Some nests do withstand the winter gales and are patched up and thickened each spring, but many are blown to pieces and the birds have to build afresh. They do seem, however, to use the same trees year after year, and many a countryman believes firmly that rooks have an uncanny instinct for knowing a sound tree, and that they will never build in a tree that is at all decayed.

The morning and evening flights of the rooks are familiar to many people. They take place because many, if not most, colonies seem to feed at some distance from their roosting-places, and the birds set off regularly every day in a long straggling procession that may stretch for some miles across the sky. Their flight is direct, with steady wing-beats, and in calm weather is often performed at considerable heights; but against strong winds the birds fly low and often break suddenly from their courses, seemingly to circumvent adverse gusts and eddies.

In spite of its familiarity the rook is the subject of a perennial controversy. Is it a friend or the enemy of the farmer and agriculturist? A great deal of time has been devoted to the study of the rook, but so complex is the problem that no definite answer has yet been given. Certain facts are established. For instance, Dr. Collinge examined the stomach contents of a large number of rooks and found that fifty-nine per cent was vegetable matter and forty-one per cent animal. Of the former, about one-third consisted of cereals and one-seventh of potatoes and other root vegetables, the remainder being made up of fruit, acorns, nuts, berries and seeds. A third of the animal matter consisted of insects, and included many injurious varieties, but nearly half of it was worms, which are, of course, of benefit to the gardener. From this one survey we see that the rook has a most varied diet and does harm as well as good, and subsequent work has emphasised the variation between rooks in different places and at different seasons. Further than this, a most exact and complete knowledge of the rook's diet would not tell us the whole truth, for, in the act of grubbing up wireworms, for example, how many young seedlings are disturbed to wither and die on the surface? Or, on the other hand, how many weeds are destroyed in like manner?

Plate 16.—The male rook arrives at the nest with his crop full of food.

Frankly, we do not yet know, but the study of the rook is still being vigorously pursued, and perhaps before long our scientists will be able to settle this age-old question.

In the course of our close-up observations of rooks we found that very little could be seen of the food. It is carried in a throat pouch just below the bill and can only be indistinctly seen as it is passed from one bird to another. It was, however, apparent that worms or large caterpillars were a prominent constituent, and on several occasions we saw two birds hold the same worm and lean back, pulling till it broke in the middle. The throat pouch, distended with food, is clearly visible in the nearest bird in Plate 16. This, the cock, has just arrived

Plate 17.—Rook feeding young.

back from a foraging expedition, and the hen, on the right, has stood up to greet him and to solicit a share of the food.

It was most interesting to notice how, especially in the early stages while the chicks were small, the food was shared out by the cock. He usually gave the first portion to his mate. Indeed, she seemed to demand it, and as soon as he arrived on the nest she grabbed his bill in hers. He then opened his gape, and she thrust her bill in and began to extract food from his crop, the whole proceeding being accompanied by an excited cawing and much shaking of the birds' heads. Soon the cock nosed the hen away, and, pushing his bill under her, he fed each of the young by regurgitation. Then perhaps the hen would be given another portion, followed by more to the chicks, and so on until his crop was exhausted. Sometimes the hen seemed not to swallow all the food she had been given, but, while the cock was feeding one of the chicks, she would re-deliver some of her portion to one of the others. The feeding process is in full swing in Plate 17, but alas! it loses a large part of its effect by not being a "talkie." Without doubt one of the most striking features of a rookery is the noise.

Minor squabbles among the members of a rookery seem to be fairly frequent, for although the birds live a community life they seem to be very jealous of intrusion into the immediate environment of their own nests. If, in the course of making its way home, a bird encroached too closely on its neighbour's preserves, there would usually be a short scuffle, with bills used as weapons, and the intruder would beat a hasty retreat. Another cause of disturbance was the comparatively common habit of the cock birds to pay undue attention to hens other than their own mates. One set of circumstances, in particular, seemed to give rise to this. When the chicks were small the hen spent most of the time brooding them, and the cock bird was accustomed to finding his mate on the nest when he returned, and, as we have described, he usually fed her. If at such a time the hen was away from the nest, the cock made no attempt to feed the chicks, but sometimes flew to another nest and tried to feed a strange hen. Normally she would not be tempted, but would attack the straying cock, striking at him with her bill.

Throughout the whole period of nesting there was a continual endeavour to strengthen or add to the nests, and twigs, pieces of straw, and feathers were frequently being brought and woven into the nest structures. The urge to find material led to a great deal of nest-robbing, and unoccupied or deserted nests were quickly pulled to pieces. In the case of nests that were temporarily unoccupied, the robbers seemed to go about their work with a guilty conscience, and they kept a careful lookout and slipped quickly away when the rightful owners put in an appearance. No doubt because of the risks of leaving the nest unattended, the majority of nests were well guarded by one or other of the adult birds until such time as the chicks were fairly well grown, and it appeared to us that while the community life may have certain advantages for the rook, the birds by no means make the best use of their opportunities.

Plate 18.—A pair of rooks at their nest.

Plate 19.—A pair of robbers look around suspiciously before taking sticks from a neighbour's nest.

Plate 20.—A rook with an elongated upper mandible.

Plate 21.—Parent rook taking pellet from young.

Plate 22.—A fight in the tree tops—an intruding rook is driven off.

The Nightingale

DARK SHADOWS dappled the moonlit path as we threaded our way one warm spring evening through a Suffolk wood. Ahead of us the tree trunks stood black against the luminous glow of the sky, and near at hand, on either side, the masses of undergrowth loomed large and forbidding. All was quiet save for the slight tread of our feet on the soft earth and the gentle murmur overhead as a light breeze stirred the soft new foliage. It was a perfect setting for the song of the nightingale, and we stepped cautiously and listened intently as we approached a part of the wood where we believed a pair of these birds to have a nest.

We were not to be disappointed, for the slight disturbance of our passage stirred the cock bird into song, and we thrilled to the soft and plaintive opening notes as they swelled through the darkness of the wood. "Pew, pew, pew, pew, pew," he began slowly, and then burst into a rich and bubbling cascade of melody that rang into the night. Phrase after phrase poured forth, resonant and sparkling, and we cautiously tiptoed our way forward towards the singer. Soon we were quite close, and we traced the nightingale to a large hawthorn near the fringe of the wood; but he was deep in the shadows and could not be seen.

Next morning we were by that way again, and we made a point of seeking out the nightingale. We listened, and soon picked out his full-throated warble among the other sounds of the wood. Rich and vibrant it certainly was, and no jot less perfect than the night before, but the effect was gone. Now he was just one voice among the many; but then, in the dark and stillness of the wood, he had held the stage, and cast a spell over the listening world.

No doubt because of his nocturnal singing the nightingale has established a remarkable reputation among the public at large. We had a clear demonstration of this during one of the war years when a nightingale sang consistently well in a wood near Derby; which is rather beyond the normal range of this bird. The fact was noted in the local paper, and in spite of the lack of transport at night, several hundred people sallied forth, some of them for considerable distances, in a pilgrimage to the haunt of Philomel.

Plate 23.—A cock nightingale.

The Robin

Of all the birds to be seen in the British Isles none can compare with the robin in popular affection. Most of us first come to hear of him in our early childhood, as, in fairy tale and nursery rhyme, he steps into our world of make-believe; but however fantastic his reputed deeds and however inaccurate our impressions of the nature of a robin's life, we do at least, through the coloured illustrations, get to know what he looks like, and there are few of us who cannot recognise the brown-clad, red-breasted robin as he perches inquisitively on the garden fence or hops to and fro in the hedge bottom and shrubbery.

Why is it that the robin has developed this unique position among our British birds? The question is difficult to answer completely, though some of the contributory reasons come readily enough to mind. In the first place the robin has a peculiarly trusting disposition towards man. Every gardener will know how the mere fact of turning over a piece of ground is enough to entice a robin into attendance; and how the robin will flit about quite close in a most engaging manner. The side of the wheelbarrow, a nearby bush, even a mound of earth, will serve him as a perch from which to watch our progress, and from time to time he will make a rapid dart close behind our spade as he catches sight of some tasty grub exposed by our digging. The housewife, too, sees the robin's confiding ways as he ventures close on to the kitchen step in response to an offering of crumbs. Yes, the robin certainly scores in that respect; but he has other attractive features as well.

The song of the robin is at once easily recognised for its clear, richly musical warble. It is a cheering song, and is all the more appreciated since it is to be heard throughout the year except for a few weeks in July and August while the birds are moulting and skulking in the undergrowth. There is no other common British bird that sings so continuously.

Finally, as a factor in the popularity of the robin, we must take account of his widespread occurrence. He is found in urban as well as country districts, and nests in woodlands and hedgerows as well as in gardens. In fact, he is everywhere, and everybody loves him.

Plate 24.—An old can makes a splendid nesting place.

The Starling

OF ALL the birds that visit the garden, surely the starling is the greatest comic. His air of bustling activity, and his rather ungainly but perky gait, serve to provide a never-failing entertainment as we watch him around the feeding-table or on the lawn. He runs here and there, probing at the ground with a vigorous thrusting of his head and long, pointed bill; always driven, it seems, by some unseen impulsive urge: and the effect is enhanced by the fact that he seldom comes alone. He brings his friends and relations to feed with him, and then squabbles furiously, jealous lest they should find some tit-bit more appetising than his morsel.

The starling is a noisy bird, both on account of the harsh, grating note that it so often uses and because it is commonly encountered in such large numbers. During the breeding season a pair of starlings may nest alone in a hole, but often the birds nest in small colonies. In any case, even during this time, starlings like to keep company, and are to be seen feeding together in flocks, squawking and whistling as they go. For the greater part of the year the starling is very strikingly gregarious, moving and feeding in flocks many hundreds strong. A flock will settle on a field and set to work with the greatest urgency, the birds seeming to fall over each other in their eagerness. Suddenly, as if at a signal, the whole flock rises with a loud whirring of wings, and swirls like a cloud of smoke blown in the wind.

It is at their roosts, particularly in the autumn and winter, that the birds can be most troublesome, for at that season our own starling population is enormously swollen by immigrants from the Low Countries and the lands around the Baltic. They come in countless thousands, or even millions, to winter in our comparatively mild climate and in the afternoons they congregate at favourite roosts in reed-beds and in spinneys. As they settle in some time before dusk they chatter very noisily, their individual voices merging into a continuous roar. Remarkable mass flights are seen at this time, as the flocks not uncommonly take to wing and wheel around before finally settling to roost. So great are the numbers that they fill the sky as a dark cloud, and the sight of such a flock helps us to appreciate what James Fisher says in his book, *Watching Birds*, that the starling is probably the most numerous of all the land birds that exist.

Plate 25.—The starling often commandeers a woodpecker's nesting place.

The Wren

Most of us are familiar with the little brown-barred, stumpy-tailed wren. He is everywhere. In woods and parklands, on overgrown wastes, and in our gardens, we find this busy, mouse-like little creature flitting to and fro, nosing among the fallen leaves and searching every nook and crevice in a search for spiders, centipedes, flies and other invertebrata which comprise the large part of his diet. He is a fascinating little bird, no less for his voice than for his industrious habits. It is a never-ending wonder that so small a creature can have so piercing and resonant a song, and it is a joy to behold him, perched on a bush, or maybe on a fence, his tail cocked perkily up over his back, and his whole frame quivering with the exuberance of the outburst.

His ball-shaped nest, with the entrance hole in the side, is usually to be found built into the shelter of a mossy bank or neatly ledged in the cleft of a tree or bush, where it fits inconspicuously with its surroundings and is not readily apparent except to experienced eyes. Such camouflage is aided in many cases by the use of indigenous material for the external layers. Thus, although dead leaves are most frequently used and suit the environment in most cases, a good deal of straw may be woven into the nest where, for example, the nesting-site is under the shelter of a thatch.

Imagine our surprise, then, when we were shown the nest that we illustrate on the opposite page. A friend was pulling up a row of broccoli plants and noticed the nest just in time to save it from destruction. There were no eggs, but he watched for a few days and presently discovered that a clutch was being laid, so, fearing the attention of his neighbours' cats, he surrounded the broccoli with wire-netting to keep them at a distance.

We were able to keep the nest under observation during the whole period of incubation and fledging, and were amused on several occasions to see sparrows feeding in the upper part of the broccoli and occasionally perching on the nest itself. When the young wrens had grown fairly big they began to take an interest in the outside world, and wondered at the disturbance on their roof. Heads popping out of the entrance hole then took the sparrows' attention, and we had the rare spectacle of a sparrow standing on top of the nest and looking down into the nest while a young wren looked out and met him face to face.

Plate 26.—The wren at her nest in a broccoli.

The Crested Tit

THE ONLY crested tits to be found in the British Isles occur in a small area of Scotland centred on the Spey Valley. In the ancient pine forests of this region the crested tit is not at all uncommon. We have seen no fewer than fifteen nests in the course of a single visit to the district, yet, only a few miles away, and over the rest of the country, the bird is quite unknown. There are, however, closely allied races to be found in many places on the Continent, and to distinguish our bird from them it is known as the Scottish Crested Tit.

The first pair of crested tits that we encountered were flitting about high up amongst the foliage of some pines. We should not have noticed them but for their call, which is similar to, and could easily be mistaken for, the call of the coal tit. We looked up and soon saw the bird that had attracted our attention. It was not unlike a coal tit in size and colour, but we could not mistake the conspicuous crest from which the bird gets its name.

We were able to watch one pair of the crested tits right through the stages of courtship, nest-building and the raising of a brood, and we found the cock to be very attentive to his mate, though, curiously enough, he was somewhat reluctant to attend to the chicks. When we first saw him he was busy collecting insects and carrying them to the hen, who was perched in a nearby tree and waited for him with quivering wings and a wide open mouth—much as a baby bird solicits food from its parents. It was then early in April. The nesting-hole was excavated by the hen, starting from a crevice in an old pine stump. Building began just before the end of the month, and though both birds worked busily at collecting material, only one seemed to do the actual building. The other, presumably the cock, just took his contributions into the hole and quickly came out again for more.

The nest was composed largely of moss, and had a scanty lining of wool and hair, and was typical of all the nests we saw of this species. Six eggs were laid and were incubated by the hen alone. Sometimes her mate came and fed her on the nest, but more often he came to call her, and the two birds went off together to feed.

The hatching of the eggs brought a climax of activity, and with it an excellent opportunity of seeing both birds of the pair, for they became exceptionally bold and fluttered round, calling all the time whenever we went near the nest. Like all the tits, they were delightful to watch, and we could not help regretting that they had so restricted a range.

Plate 27.—The crested tit.

The Willow-Tit

THE WILLOW-TIT provides an interesting example of the value of field observations to supplement laboratory and museum study in the recognition and classification of birds. It occurs locally in small numbers in most parts of Great Britain, yet in spite of this widespread distribution it was not identified as a species distinct from the marsh-tit until the beginning of the present century.

The two birds are very similar in plumage, and are like the better-known coal tit except that they lack the white patch on the nape. Both of them have the characteristic black crown and black throat. The cheeks are whitish, merging to a bluff-white on the sides of the neck and the underparts, while the wings and back are brown, slightly tinged with olive green.

With the growth of the study of birds as living creatures, the one striking dissimilarity between the two species was brought to light. The willow-tit has markedly different call notes from those of the marsh-tit. Whereas the latter frequently uses a note well described in the *Handbook of British Birds* as "pitchuu," the willow-tit never uses this note. It uses a thin, sibilant "eez, eez, eez," and a high pitched "zi-zi-zi-zi," which are not included in the marsh-tits' repertoire. One note the two birds have in common is a sound often written as "tchaa-tchaa-tchaa," but even with this there is a difference in that the note rendered by the willow-tit is much harsher and more grating than that of the marsh-tit.

As soon as attention was thus directed to the difference of species, certain other distinguishing features came to be recognised. Among these, close inspection of the plumage established the fact that the crown of the willow-tit is a dull, sooty colour whereas the crown of the marsh-tit is a deep, glossy black; and the latter has a smooth, well-groomed appearance which is lacking in the case of the willow-tit. Another distinction is that the willow-tit has buff edges to the wing secondaries which show as a light patch when the wing is closed.

The marsh- and willow-tits are rather similar in their habitats, nesting as a rule in soft, rotten stumps of willows, alders, and birches; but whereas the marsh-tit usually uses a natural hole, the willow-tit, starting with an existing crevice, excavates its own nesting-hole, and in spite of the suggestion conveyed by the names, the willow-tit shows a decided preference for damp, marshy woods and copses, whereas the marsh-tit is to be found equally in dry as well as wet places.

In flight and general habits the willow-tit and the marsh-tit are very similar to the well-known great tit, and it is not unlikely that the birds are often overlooked by many people, and that their occurrence is in fact more frequent than is often supposed.

Plate 28.—The willow-tit.

The Stone-Curlew

On the sandy heaths of East Suffolk we found several pairs of stone-curlews during the breeding season of 1945. It was our first opportunity since 1936 to resume the study of these birds, and we were interested to compare them with those we had previously seen and recorded.* There was, of course, a general similarity of behaviour, and the thrill of close acquaintance with these long-legged plovers came back to us as strongly as ever; and as, from the confines of our hide, we watched their cautious approaches to the nest, we recalled vividly our earlier experiences.

The nest we now illustrate contained two comparatively fresh eggs when we found it in early May, and they must have been about ten days old when we began our detailed observations. However, in spite of the relatively early stage of the incubation, the parent stone-curlews seemed completely uninfluenced by the presence of the hide, and the hen was back on the nest within fifteen minutes of the start of our first spell of watching. As she stood over the eggs, we admired again the neat beauty of the flecked sandy plumage, the conspicuous light wing-bar, and the fascinating large yellow eye that is so characteristic of this bird. She settled quickly and soon appeared to be dozing, and, except for two slight changes of position, she remained thus for the whole of the three and a half hours we stayed in the hide.

We had seen nothing of the male stone-curlew during that first watch, but a few days later he was much more in evidence. There is no regular difference in plumage between the sexes, but, as is not unusual among birds, minor differences between individuals enable us to distinguish them from others of their kind, and in this case one bird, which we were able to identify as the cock, was markedly lighter in colour than the other. It was this light-coloured bird which made the first approach to the nest during our second spell in the hide. Only ten minutes after we had settled down he alighted on the ground about twenty yards away. We watched him eagerly, and saw how, first of all, he stretched up to his full height and looked about him. Reassured, he came forward a few quick steps, his body now lowered to a horizontal poise and his head extended well forward. He halted to look around him, and then came on again, making a zigzag track towards the nest. He settled at once on to the eggs, but, seeming uncomfortable, got up, walked around a few paces, and then settled down again, this time in earnest. He had been brooding about an hour when the hen called from a little way off. At this we looked up and saw her running round in a large circle. The cock immediately left the nest and ran rapidly towards his mate. As he reached her, he opened his wings and

* *Intimate Sketches from Bird Life*, Chap. 3.

[*Continued on page 52.*

Plate 29.—The stone-curlew returns to incubate the eggs.

Plate 30.—The first chick is hatched.

Plate 31.—The cock stone-curlew returns with food for the first hatched chick.

ran off at an angle. We were just beginning to think that this was done in display, when a stoat ran out from the shelter of a nearby gorse bush. The cock stone-curlew instantly leapt into the air, and, calling vigorously, mobbed the stoat. As the bird dived down, the stoat jumped up at him, leaping almost two feet off the ground; but the blow missed its mark, and the stoat bounded off and disappeared under another bush, and so probably into one of the many rabbit-holes that honeycomb the heath.

It was noticeable during most of the incubation period that, although both cock and hen took turns at brooding the eggs, the change-over occurred some little distance from the nest. With the approach of the hatch, however, and particularly after the eggs had begun to chip, the sitting bird seemed more loath to go off duty and usually remained at the nest until the relieving bird had actually arrived. The whole attitude of these birds is so intense at this period that it is well worth the effort, on the part of anybody who is interested, to spend some time in a hide during these two or three critical days.

It was on May 30th that the first egg hatched. This occurred shortly after the cock had taken over a spell of duty at the nest, and although the fact may

Plate 32.—A young stone-curlew waits beside the cock.

Plate 33.—The hen feeds one of the chicks while the cock continues to brood.

have no special significance, it is curious to notice that each time we have observed the emergence of a stone-curlew chick the brooding bird has been the cock. In this case he fidgeted on the eggs, but did not assist the hatching by inserting his bill into the egg as we described in *Intimate Sketches from Bird Life.* He brooded the chick and the unhatched egg, but soon began picking up small fragments of the empty shell and eating them, and he kept up a continuous "conversation" with the newly hatched chick. He remained on the nest for about two hours and the hen meantime settled herself about twenty yards away and spent some of her time in preening. The birds were then disturbed by some one who walked across the heath, and they both ran a little way and then flew out of sight; but the cock was back within five minutes and resumed his brooding, which continued without disturbance until we left the hide after a six-hour vigil.

We set out again early the next morning and found the second egg not yet

[*Continued on page* 56.

Plate 34. In this case the food was placed on the ground immediately in front of the chick.

Plate 35. The chick seeks warmth under the cock's body.

hatched, but with quite a large hole in the end of it. The hen was soon back to brood, and the cock arrived shortly afterwards and spent some time wandering around and picking at the ground as if feeding. Several times he came right up to the nest as if anxious to take over, but the hen would not leave, and he contented himself with bringing small morsels for the previously hatched chick, which was now quite strong, and ran out to meet him when he called. He would drop the food on the ground immediately in front of the chick, and then point to it with his bill until the chick found it.

Presently, however, the cock came back in a different manner. This time there was no food for the chick, but as he approached he kept stopping and picking up small stones and rabbit droppings and casting them aside over his shoulder. As he neared the nest, the hen stood up and moved away, and we saw that the second chick was on the point of hatching. He quickly settled over the half-hatched chick, but had hardly done so when he stood up again, picked up the empty eggshell and ran from the nest with it. He must have run thirty yards, shaking the shell from side to side as he went and breaking it into pieces. He ate the main piece and picked up some of the scraps that he had dropped, and then hurried back to the nest. He now brooded both chicks while the hen collected

Plate 36.—The young stone-curlew leaves the nest.

Plate 37.—Both chicks are hatched and the parents are kept busy feeding them.

food for the elder one, but after about half an hour the parents changed over again.

During the afternoon feeding became much more rapid, and this and the brooding were completely shared by the adults. Much of the food was found quite close to the nest, and it was interesting to see how these birds approached their quarry stealthily and then caught it by a sudden quick jab. In this way even flies and blue-bottles were caught without difficulty.

By early evening the second chick was beginning to gain strength, and after a period of brooding the cock got up off the nest and then settled down about two feet away. Both chicks scrambled across to get under him, but as they did so he got up and moved a little further. So they were led off gradually into the shelter of some nettles, and we terminated one of the most interesting days we have ever spent in quest of birds.

The Lapwing

THERE IS something exhilarating about the apparently carefree nuptial flight of the lapwing. With a sudden erratic beat disturbing the otherwise slow flapping action of the large, rounded wings, the bird lurches hither and thither. It throws itself about in aerial evolutions that suggest momentarily that it is out of control; but then, with a quick swoop near the ground, it demonstrates an amazing mastery of the power of flight.

Even the ordinary everyday flights of the lapwing are marked by an erratic action so characteristic that the bird can be identified at a considerable distance by this one feature.

The lapwing is by far the most familiar of our waders, for it habitually frequents arable land and is found in all parts of the British Isles. It is with us

Plate 38.—The lapwing at her nest.

Plate 39.—Lapwing's nest containing five eggs and a chick.

throughout the year, and although in winter some of our birds do move south to the Atlantic seaboard of Europe, the ranks of those that remain are very greatly swelled by winter visitors from the Low Countries and the lands around the Baltic. For the greater part of the year great flocks of lapwings are a common sight, for the bird is very sociable; and farmers may well feel pleased if the flocks descend in their fields, for, with the possible exception of the barn owl, there is no bird that is of more value to the agriculturist. Its food consists very largely of injurious insects, including the all-too-prevalent wire-worm.

It might be expected that, in the case of so common a bird as the lapwing, there would be nothing new to discover in the course of field observations; yet, only recently, we came on a remarkable nest with six eggs—the first time so large a clutch has been recorded for this bird.

The Redshank

THE dominant voice on many a coarse grassy marshland, particularly near the sea coast, is undoubtedly that of the redshank. As soon as we intrude on to the edge of one of these boggy wastes, his is the call we expect to hear first; a strident "tooee-tooee-tooee," as the bird takes wing at the very first indication of danger. He has well been called "the sentinel of the marshes." We see him flying round in wide circles; a swift flight on powerful, long, and pointed wings, with a conspicuous white band showing along the trailing edges.

The redshank is a shy and restless bird, and we must be patient if we are to see him closely. We conceal ourselves on the marsh, and gradually confidence returns to its wild denizens; but as the redshank was the first to be alarmed, so he is one of the last to settle and resume his feeding. We watch him plane down and alight on a fence-post. His finely-shaped wings are poised gracefully above his back for a moment, and we see the gleaming white of his underparts. He folds his wings and stands there looking about him. His grey-brown flecked plumage is smart but not striking, but if the light is good we notice the reddish-orange colour of his longish legs, from which, of course, he gets his name.

Although the redshank is most common on coastal marshes and spends much time feeding around the shores of muddy estuaries, a great many of the birds move inland during the spring and nest in wet meadows, especially in the neighbourhood of large, slow-flowing rivers.

The nest is usually well concealed in a tuft of coarse grass, and the grasses are drawn together over it to form a kind of thatch, which conceals the eggs from observation by predators and gives the sitting bird some protection against wind and rain. But this is not an essential characteristic, for some nests are situated in shorter grass where no cover is possible. Like most of the ground-nesting birds, the redshank alights some little way off and makes her way cautiously to the nest, and it is during this approach that we have been able to secure some of our best pictures of the bird.

Plate 40.—The redshank makes her way cautiously to the nest.

The Ring-Ouzel

WITHIN the family of birds that might be designated as "thrushes," that is, the genus "turdus," there are some remarkable differences as well as some striking similarities. The two commonest in this country, the song-thrush and the blackbird, are both largely sedentary. Some do migrate to Ireland or to France, but many are resident with us the whole year round. The redwing and the fieldfare, on the other hand, occur in most parts of these islands only as winter visitors from their breeding haunts in Northern Europe; while the ring-ouzel is a summer visitor, breeding here, and then migrating to the Mediterranean region for the winter.

The ring-ouzel is often called the "mountain blackbird," for in many respects it is very like its better-known cousin. It is similar in build, and has the same deliberate, contemplative habits when on the ground, and lifts and spreads its tail in the same characteristic manner on alighting; but the emphasis must be on "mountain," for it is unusual to find the ring-ouzel nesting much below the 1000-ft. line. Its typical haunts are the high moors of the Pennines and North-East Yorkshire, and the hilly uplands of Scotland and Wales, and of Devon and Cornwall.

We took our photographs on the Yorkshire Pennines—a wild, desolate moorland region, so inhospitable in winter that the keeper up there was snowed up for nine weeks in 1941, and, with his telephone wires broken down by the weight of the snow, he was so completely isolated from the outside world that he must have perished but for the provisions stored in his cottage. Even in March, when the ring-ouzel returns from migration, the moors are exceedingly bleak, and one needs to be warmly clad to go out watching for early ring-ouzels.

When we were in Yorkshire in 1943 we were surprised at the comparative abundance of ring-ouzels. They seemed to be far more numerous than in their other breeding haunts, and, and assisted by Messrs. George Edwards and Edward Watson, we found ten nests in the strip of moorland where we were working; and there must have been several others, for we did not make an exhaustive search. The area was about two miles by a quarter mile.

Nesting begins in early April, for one nest that we saw had young chicks in it on the twentieth; but not all ring-ouzels start so early, and later in the season we found nests in all stages of development. One nest still had eggs at the end of June, but this was probably a second brood, two broods being not uncommon for the species.

A feature that rather astonished us was the variety of nesting sites. Taking account of all the ring-ouzels we have seen in their various breeding haunts, it is safe to say that the most usual site is a niche among the tussocks on the steep

[*Continued on page 64.*

Plate 41. The ring-ouzel nests among moorland tussocks.

Plate 42. The ring-ouzel or mountain blackbird.

side of a moorland ravine or the bank of a moorland stream, but rocky outcrops are also much favoured. Old walls and derelict farm buildings are readily used, and in the Yorkshire area to which we referred, these old buildings accounted for a large proportion of the nests. The building of reservoirs has led to the compulsory abandonment of several farms in the vicinity, and, particularly where the roofs have fallen in, ring-ouzels have built their nests in the niches left in the walls by the fallen timbers. The birds seem to prefer open, light interiors, though we did find one nest on the mantelpiece in a disused living-room where the roof was complete and access was by the windows.

One of the nests that we illustrate was somewhat unusual in that it was situated among bracken on a steep bank. From this it seems that the type of vegetation around the nest does not matter. It may be heather, coarse grass

Plate 43.—A ring-ouzel's nest among bracken.

or bracken; or there may be none at all, as in the case of the nests in the buildings.

As our photographs show, the distinguishing mark of the adult ring-ouzel is very plain to see. It has a whitish crescent-shaped marking on the breast which shows up clearly against the sooty colour of the rest of the plumage; but some care must be taken in the identification, because blackbirds are rather prone to albinism, and a pied blackbird might easily be mistaken for a ring-ouzel. A further distinguishing feature is that many of the wing feathers of the ring-ouzel are conspicuously light on the edges, so that the closed wing itself appears much lighter than the rest of the body. The song is also quite distinct, for the ring-ouzel has none of the sweet-flowing melody of the blackbird, but limits himself to the repetition of a single note or pair of notes.

The Twite

THE TWITE, which is also sometimes called the "mountain linnet," is not uncommon in Scotland and the Hebrides where it nests in open rough country and on bracken-clad hillsides; but in England it is very local, and is practically confined to the heather moors of the northern half of the country.

It was in the course of working on the ring-ouzel that we noticed a party of a score or so twites feeding on an enclosed piece of ploughed land on the fringe of the moors. Most of them were searching the ground, but twos and threes were sitting on the black stone walls, and some were singing their linnet-like song. Gradually, in small parties, they flew away towards a rocky outcrop, and suspecting this as a likely nesting-place, we made a note to follow up the clue.

That evening we explored the region of the outcrop without discovering the twites, but while we were searching a nearby patch of heather a twite flew out, and Mr. George Edwards, who was with us, quickly found the nest. During the next few days we found another four nests, all in the same patch of heather, and all containing five or six eggs.

We selected one of the nests for photography and were charmed by the response of the birds. Seldom have we worked on such tame or fearless creatures. The eggs had now hatched, and even while we were getting into the hide and erecting the camera, both the old birds came back to the nest and fed the chicks. That finished, the cock flew on to the top of the hide and sang there for several minutes; and while he sang the hen flew up, and she perched, of all places, on the camera lens hood, which was, by then, projecting out of the front of the hide.

In the course of our observations it was interesting to note that a second cock was paying his attentions to the hen at this nest. He would wait until the rightful cock had gone off to collect food, and then, flying down to some vantage point, very often our hide, he would sing vigorously for a few moments before dropping down into the heather close by the nest. He made several advances to the hen, but she would have none of it, and thrust her head forward at him with beak open, and when he came close she pecked at him viciously. Over and over again this went on until the rightful cock returned and drove off the intruder.

Plate 44.—In Northern England the twite nests on heather moors.

The Black-headed Gull

IT USED to be said, and the superstition dies hard and is still heard in places, that the presence of gulls inland foretold a hard winter or was a sign of stormy weather at sea. There is just a germ of truth hidden in the idea, because some gulls do undoubtedly move inland during very severe weather; but they only add slightly to the already large population of gulls that are to be found in many inland localities at all times of the year.

The most common of these inland-breeding gulls is the black-headed gull. It nests in large colonies, usually in swampy and boggy places near lakes and rivers, making its nest on a tussock of grass or sometimes on small prominences or islands standing up out of shallow water. Some of these nesting sites are many miles from the sea, as, for instance, a large one high up on the Yorkshire Pennines above Halifax, where we took the picture reproduced on the opposite page. The gulls are very bold in defence of their nests, and many times as we have been walking in their vicinity the birds have dived aggressively at us, swerving from the attack only at the last moment and flashing by only a foot or two above our heads. Such attacks are quite unpleasant experiences until one gets accustomed to them and realises their limitations.

The black-headed gull is a familiar bird to many people, but it is not always recognised for what it is. The dark head, which, by the way, is really a rich chocolate colour and not black at all, is the spring and summer plumage, and while this lasts the bird is readily identified; but the dark hood is shed in the moult, and in autumn and winter the bird's head is white and merely blotched to a variable extent with greyish-brown markings. If, at such a time, some further identification is needed, it is to be found in the blood-red bill and legs which are characteristic of the black-headed gull.

It is not easy to say whether the black-headed gull is beneficial or otherwise to agriculture, though, on the whole, it appears that it is. The diet is very varied and depends largely on what is available. The bird readily takes an opportunity to follow the plough and picks up worms and other invertebrates, including large numbers of injurious species such as wire-worms and leather-jackets. Some seeds and roots are also eaten, and the bird is a voracious scavenger. Many black-headed gulls frequent towns and large cities, feeding on sewage farms and open spaces, but also keeping open a keen eye for scraps, and the Thames Embankment and the London parks would be less interesting if it were not for their presence in large numbers.

Plate 45.—Black-headed gulls nesting on a Yorkshire reservoir.

The Common Curlew

AMONG the sensory factors that stimulate the memory, sound, in some of of its manifestations, is a most powerful agent for producing vivid recollections. This is particularly true of some natural sounds, especially those heard in wild or lonely places, though it is probably true of any sound that can convey a mood. Thus the roaring of the sea, or the howling of the wind, may bring to mind some bygone occasion, and present it more vividly than could a visual reminder of the same event.

Some bird calls exemplify this phenomenon, and of these there can hardly be a more striking example than the wild, exhilarating note of the curlew. The sound of it, even from a gramophone record, takes us back immediately to the haunts in which we have studied this bird, and we think especially of some of the upland swamps of Central Wales, where the curlew nests in considerable numbers. The district around Llandrindod Wells is one of our happy hunting grounds, and we always approach it with our ears tuned for the rising, bubbling trill that voices the spirit of these hills. There is a ringing keenness in the curlew's song, and yet, withal, a haunting, mystic strain that captures the imagination and impels us on to seek the bird from whence it comes.

The nest is not usually difficult to find, though it is often well sheltered among tufty grass or heather. The curlew nests on dry moors and rough pastures as well as in boggy places, but the nest is seldom far from a swamp, for the bird feeds largely in soft, oozy mud. The long, curved bill is sensitive at the tip, and is thrust deep into the mud to probe for larvæ, beetles, slugs, and small frogs, or for any other creature that may be hidden there. It will be noticed that the bird's nostrils are located well up towards the base of the bill so that breathing is not interrupted by the search for food.

An interesting feature that is clearly shown in our photographs is that the bill of the curlew varies considerably in length. Some birds have bills as short as four or five inches, while others must measure quite eight inches.

The eggs are large and rounded at one end and taper sharply towards the other, so that four of them, which is a normal clutch, fit closely together in the shallow scraping that serves as a nest. They vary considerably in their colour and may range from a stone colour to quite a deep brown, or they may have a distinct greenish tinge; and the markings vary between brown, buff and grey, and sometimes take the form of large blotches, and at other times are merely spots and scrolls of various sizes.

Regular incubation does not begin until the clutch is complete, so that, although the eggs are laid at intervals over a week or more, and incubation lasts about thirty days, yet the chicks usually hatch within a very short time of

[*Continued on page 74.*

Plate 46.—Some curlews have particularly long bills.

Plate 47.—The eggs are chipped. At this stage we can hear the chicks squeaking inside the shells.

Plate 48.—The curlew chicks in the act of hatching.

Plate 49.—The curlew dries her newly-hatched chicks.

each other. We have usually found that only about three or four hours separate the emergence of the first and last chick. This is an extraordinary provision of Nature to enable the curlew to deal with her young family, for no sooner are the chicks dry than they are out of the nest, darting and staggering hither and thither among the grass, and requiring the active attention of their parents to guard them and to keep them supplied with food.

To sit in a hide close by a curlew's nest during the hatching period is a really fascinating experience. The hen becomes very agitated with excitement as she sits on the eggs. She keeps fidgeting and shuffling, and from time to time thrusts her bill down under her breast and seems to move the eggs a little. Presently we can hear the young chicks squeaking from inside their shells. They have worked round the large ends of the eggs, tapping and chipping them from the inside with the little bony projections on their bills, and soon first one and then another punctures the shell and makes a hole. Their calls increase in intensity and the hen answers them with evident emotion. The chick continues working, and the hole is extended along the line of the crack until eventually the chick is able to push the end off the shell and to struggle out to freedom.

The hen probably gets up for a moment to look down at the chick, but she soon settles again to brood it till it is dry, fussing underneath herself from time to time to attend to her offspring. Soon the second, the third, and the fourth are hatched, and as each becomes dry, the buff and black downy little creatures push out their heads and then their bodies from under the hen, and with surprising agility for such young creatures they scamper about around the nest and soon make their way into the surrounding grass.

Plate 50.—The curlew family moves into the surrounding grass.

The Cuckoo

EVER SINCE man took an interest in birds the cuckoo has been notorious and at the same time a creature of mystery. Its penetrating and monotonous voice breaks into the general chorus of bird-song about the middle of April, and, whether we care or not, the fact is driven home to us that the cuckoo has arrived. His striking notes permit of no confusion, save with the mimicking practical joker who would sometimes have us believe that the cuckoo is before his time; and the very simplicity of the disyllabic call makes it known and recognised by every one.

The strange behaviour of the cuckoo raises many interesting problems. Why should it, alone among our British birds, rely on other species to rear its young? How does the cuckoo deposit its egg into nests which are comparatively inaccessible to it? By what means is the colour of the egg evolved so that it often closely matches the eggs of the foster-parent? And how do young cuckoos, travelling some weeks after the adults have left, find their way on migration to Africa? We cannot pretend to explain all the mysteries of the cuckoo, though we can recommend two books* by men who have given many years to the study of this fascinating bird and have written most interesting accounts of their researches. We can, however, contribute a series of photographs which illustrate one phase of the young cuckoo's existence, and the incident we witnessed seems worth describing.

It was during the summer of 1945 that we were out with a Suffolk gamekeeper who has an extensive knowledge of the small wild birds as well as of those that more directly affect his vocation, when we noticed a tree pipit singing on the top of a post. Several times it made short aerial sallies and returned again to its perch, and we were struck by the vigour of its song. As we watched, it flew down to the ground and was lost to sight among the bilberry, for its territory was a strip of heathland fringed by a wood. After a few moments it was up again on the wing and flew across to an oak, where it alighted on a bough. We brought our glasses to bear, and saw that it was jerking its head, apparently flogging a caterpillar in the manner common to many insectivorous birds; and having killed the caterpillar to its satisfaction, it flew down to the ground with it.

Here, surely, was evidence of a nest with the hen sitting very close, so we searched the vicinity, and after some time succeeded in flushing the hen tree pipit. Several times we must have beaten the herbage within a few feet of her, yet she had not flown, and when we looked into the nest we saw the reason why. One egg had just hatched. We looked again. The chick was not at all like a young

* *The Truth about the Cuckoo*, Edgar Chance (*Country Life*, 1940). *Cuckoo Problems*, Stuart Baker (Witherby, 1942).

[*Continued on page 80.*

Plate 51.—The tree-pipit that acted as foster mother to the young cuckoo.

Plates 52 and 53 (overleaf).—Stages in the ejection of the tree-pipit's eggs by the young cuckoo.

tree-pipit. It was devoid of all down and was a dull leaden colour. Surely it was a young cuckoo.

At intervals we visited the nest to see when the young cuckoo would begin its foul work of ejecting the tree-pipit's eggs, but nothing happened that day. Next morning the three eggs were still in the nest, and so they were at midday; but at 2 p.m., when we returned, we found one egg was lying outside the nest. The cuckoo was then about twenty-eight hours old.

Wanting to record the whole sequence of events we carefully replaced the egg, and opened up the nest a little to facilitate photography. Presently the young cuckoo seemed to come suddenly to life. The eggs pressing against its sides were irritating it. It wriggled about in the nest and wormed its way backwards under one of the eggs. With some difficulty it managed to get the egg on to its back, and held it there by raising the two embryo wings, as can be seen clearly in several of the series of pictures. Then began the struggle. Resting on the point of its bill, and pushing with its long legs, it slowly forced itself up the side of the nest. Every now and then it paused, took a fresh grip with its feet, and then heaved again. Right up the side of the nest and over the rim it went, and we were surprised to see how far the young cuckoo continued to push the egg. It seemed that it continued pushing until the egg fell away from off its back—an event which was somewhat delayed in the present instance because the surrounding ground was level with the rim of the nest and continued to support the egg.

The young cuckoo seemed exhausted after its efforts, and lay still for a little while before attempting to regain the nest, but before long it wriggled back and appeared to go to sleep.

We retreated some distance in case the tree-pipits should be wanting to return, and soon we saw them come down and feed the cuckoo. It slept again after this for about half an hour, and then, on awakening, began to dispose of the second egg. The procedure was very similar to that just described, and the egg was left close to the first one. The third egg followed in like manner, and the cuckoo was left alone in possession of the nest.

When we went away we took charge of the discarded eggs in order to carry out an experiment. We replaced them in the nest with the cuckoo the following morning to see what would happen. They were pushed out again as before. On the fourth day we tried again, and once again they were ejected; but when we repeated the test on the fifth day the cuckoo had lost its urge to dispose of the eggs, and they remained in the nest until we removed them twenty-four hours later. Thus the ejection impulse lasted only during the second, third and fourth days of the cuckoo's existence.

The cuckoo grew rapidly, and at a week old it so filled the nest that, even had the tree-pipit's eggs been allowed to hatch, the chicks would have stood no

[*Continued on page 83.*

Plate 54.—A young cuckoo being fed by a meadow-pipit.

Plate 55.—A young cuckoo ready for flight.

chance of survival, but would have been crushed, suffocated or starved by the interloper.

As we show in Plate 54 the cuckoo's gape was enormous compared with that of its foster-parent, and the tree-pipit had a busy time satisfying its appetite. The situation rapidly becomes almost fantastic, for the fledgling quite outstrips the birds that are so busily attending it, and by the time it is ready to leave the nest at about three weeks old it is quite twice as large as they are.

The Whinchat

WHAT a delightful, perky bird the whinchat is. His rather dapper plumage and his insistent scolding when we enter his domain bring him to our attention when he might otherwise pass unnoticed. He is a bird of the roadside wastes and of rough pastures and commons; of places, in fact, where coarse, tufted grass gives him the shelter he so much likes for his nest.

In such situations the whinchat occurs throughout the British Isles, being comparatively numerous in some places, yet rather scarce in others, and seeming to vary somewhat in distribution from year to year. Thus, in parts of South Derbyshire, where he was seldom noticed a few years ago, the whinchat has been comparatively common during the last two years.

The whinchat is a summer visitor, arriving here towards the end of April or in early May, and leaving again in September. It is during the first two months of this period that we see and hear him most, for his song falls off after about the end of June. During those two months, however, which include the periods of nest-building, incubation and fledging of the young, we see the whinchat repeatedly as we move about the lanes and byways. He perches on the topmost branch of a bush and sings his warbling little song, interrupting it every now and again to scold us with a sharp "tic, tic." The posts of wire fences by the roadside are another favourite perch, and in the vicinity of the nest, we see him and his mate flitting to and fro and perching and swaying on tall grasses, or the old, dead stems of last year's docks and other similar weeds.

It is, indeed, this tendency to perch on almost anything handy that makes the whinchat particularly easy to photograph, for if a suitable perch is placed near the birds' route back to the nest, the chances are that both cock and hen will use it and will pose for us as we show on the opposite page.

Plate 56.—The whinchat readily used the perch we provided for him.

The Kingfisher

FAMILIAR though the kingfisher is in name and appearance, it is surprisingly seldom seen by most people. Its familiarity must have been achieved by means of coloured illustrations, the bird being not infrequently depicted because of its striking colours. Thus most of us are aware of the kingfisher as a rather stumpy, short-tailed bird with a large, strong bill, and we know that he has a reddish-orange breast and a bluish-green back.

Actually the kingfisher is fairly plentiful, and is well distributed throughout the British Isles in places where streams or lakes provide it with facilities for fishing and the banks are suitable for nesting; but the bird is shy and retiring, and, as a rule, keeps well out of sight. In fact, when we do see it at all it is usually only a bluish-green streak flashing quickly by, and rapidly disappearing from view.

In spite of its shyness, however, the kingfisher is an easy bird to watch if we set about our watching the right way. He is a bird of regular habits, and has certain favourite perches from which he watches the water beneath for fish and aquatic insects; and if we erect a hiding-tent near to one of these perches, and enter it with the determination to be patient, we shall, sooner or later, get a close-up view of this strikingly handsome avian fisher.

A swift, direct flight, close above the water, brings him to the chosen perch. On alighting he may turn a time or two, but then, sitting in an erect pose, he will keep remarkably still except for an occasional turn of the head. Suddenly he spies a likely-looking victim, and he drops quickly with a splash into the water, to return a moment later with a writhing fish held firmly in his bill. A large fish is often flogged to stun or kill it before it is swallowed, but small creatures are swallowed direct.

The kingfisher is resident in this country throughout the year, and may, accordingly, be watched at any time, but he is, of course, forced to forsake some of his haunts when the water becomes ice-bound, and he is then to be found around the coast, feeding below the tide-line in rocky pools and shallow channels.

Plate 57.—The kingfisher.

Montagu's Harrier

IN *Birds of the Day* we described some experiences with the marsh-harrier, and referred to it as the rarest of the birds that breed regularly in the British Isles. Now comes the turn of its near relative, the Montagu's harrier. This also is a rare bird, but, because it is less timid than the marsh-harrier, and, unlike that bird, does not confine itself exclusively to marsh-land, it finds more areas acceptable as possible breeding-sites, and is, therefore, not quite so restricted in range or numbers. In addition to Norfolk, which, by virtue of its large areas of reedy marsh is the county most favoured by the harriers, the Montagu's harrier is often to be found nesting in Suffolk, Cambridge, Hampshire, and the South-West of England, and in South Wales, and occasionally also in some other parts of the country; but, curiously enough, it does not occur in the North or in Scotland, although a very similar bird, the hen-harrier, breeds regularly in the Orkneys.

Montagu's harrier arrives here in April, after having wintered in Tropical or South Africa, or possibly even as far afield as India or Burma; but apparently it does not settle at once into its breeding haunts, as, at least in Norfolk, where we have for the most part watched this bird, it is seldom in evidence before the middle of May. From then onwards it may be seen in suitable places, but only in small numbers, and we consider ourselves fortunate if we see more than a single pair.

It was while we were working on a pair of short-eared owls that were nesting on a marsh near the sea coast that we saw a cock Montagu's harrier mobbing the hen short-eared owl. He dived at her repeatedly, but she adroitly swerved each time to miss his attacks, and we noticed that, good a performer as the Montagu's harrier undoubtedly is on the wing, he was no match for the owl. She could outmanœuvre him every time. Our interest was immediately roused, as it was then towards the end of May—time for the Montagu's harrier to have settled down to nesting—and this was the first one we had seen in the district for some years.

During the next few days we kept a look-out for further signs of the harrier and saw him hunting across the marsh on several occasions, but it was not until June 3rd that we caught a glimpse of a hen, and then we were unable to follow up the clue. On June 9th we saw a pair of harriers together, and, watching them closely through binoculars, we followed their movements, taking particular note of the hen. She dropped down into the reeds and we watched intently, making a mental note of the location; but in a few moments she was up again, this time with a piece of sedge in her bill. Now we watched more keenly still, and presently we saw her alight on a marsh about a mile from

[*Continued on page 92.*

Plate 58.—The hen Montagu's harrier hovering in flight.

Plate 59.—The cock Montagu's harrier visits the hen at the nest.

Plate 60.—The hen watching the cock as he flies away from the nest.

where we stood. This was unfamiliar ground to us; much intersected by deep dykes, and not readily traversed in a straight line; so we took careful bearings on the position and then set out to find the nest.

The marsh was covered with a dense growth of sedge, which made searching difficult, so when we came close to where we calculated the nest should be, we spread out to cover as wide a front as possible and then walked forward, hoping to flush the harrier. We had not gone far when suddenly the hen flew up just ahead of us and we located the nest without difficulty. It consisted of a rather deep, round mat of sedge, some two feet across, well hollowed in the centre to cradle the three eggs, which, we noticed, were very white and clean and appeared to be quite fresh.

The nest was on ground belonging to Major Anthony Buxton, who is himself a keen ornithologist, so at the first convenient opportunity we went to see him to ask permission to erect a hide and photograph these birds. This permission was readily granted, but Major Buxton surprised us by saying that he had already found the nest himself. We went together to inspect it, and then found, to our greater astonishment, that this was not the nest we had found. There were, then, two nests, each with three eggs, within a few hundred yards of each other—yet nobody had seen two pairs of Montagu's harriers about in the vicinity! Was this another case of polygamy as we had already noted in the case of the marsh-harrier?

We erected our hide and settled down to work, and at once we found that here was as perfect a pair of Montagu's as we could hope to encounter. True, our preparations had been carefully made, but even so we could hardly have hoped for the response we got. On the very first occasion that we occupied the hide, the hen was back on the nest within nine minutes, and she showed not the slightest trace of suspicion or nervousness. The first egg had just hatched, and the hen shuffled the chick and the two other eggs into position and settled down comfortably to brood them.

This first really close-up view of the hen Montagu's harrier was a fascinating spectacle. Her dark, lustrous eye was especially striking, being accentuated by the light buff-coloured patch surrounding it. Her finely-shaped head was beautifully flecked with brown on a buff background, and this fleck marking extended also on to the neck and breast, and, to a certain extent, on to the flanks. Her back and wings were a dark brown, but the feathers were individually beautiful, with various amounts of lighter brown or buff around the edges and at the tips; and the tail was finely barred in shades of brown, the outer feathers showing conspicuous bars of quite light buff when the tail was spread.

There was very little activity on the nest during this first watch, as the hen was primarily engaged in brooding, but every now and again she shuffled a little to change her position, and sometimes did a little preening, stretched a

[*Continued on page 94.*

Plate 61.—The young line up to be fed.

wing, or tugged idly at the nest lining to while away the time. Once she stood up on the nest and gazed down at the small chick. It squeaked feebly at her as if asking for food, and she looked around the nest as if looking for something to give the chick; but, finding nothing, she pulled a small soft feather from her shoulder and offered that to the youngster. The feather was accepted and swallowed, and the hen settled down again to brood.

All was very quiet on the nest for about two hours, when suddenly the hen got up and left to the accompaniment of a shrill screaming note. We had not noticed any call from the cock, but it soon became obvious that he was close overhead. We saw the hen meet him in the air, take something from him, and then, still screaming, return quickly to the nest. She brought a young pheasant chick in her talons, and stood on the edge of the nest for a few moments, clutching it tightly and still screaming excitedly to the cock. She kept up this vigorous calling until the cock flew away, when she turned round on the nest, took a fresh grip on the prey, and began to tear it to pieces with strong upward pulls. She swallowed each piece herself and offered none to the chick, and when she had taken her fill she resumed brooding.

We saw no food given to the chick during a three-hour watch, neither was there any food on the nest when we visited it the next morning. The second egg had then hatched and the third was well chipped. It may have hatched later that day, for the chick was dry and lively when we saw it the following morning.

On our arrival at the hide on that occasion we had quite a surprise. The Montagu's harrier usually builds its nest low down; supported on sedge, but only just off the ground. On this marsh, however, the sedge was so dense that, as will be seen in the photographs, the nest was raised on a fairly thick cushion. Now, in preparing for photography, we had trampled the sedge between the nest and the hide, and, with the emergence of the chicks, the harrier had taken the opportunity to build a new, but rather rough, nest on this beaten-down sedge, and had transferred the chicks to this new nest. Interesting as this incident was, it did not suit our plans at all, so we replaced the chicks in the original nest, where there was, by the way, the remains of a small leveret, and retired to the edge of the marsh to watch events. We saw the harrier return to her nest within a few minutes and stay down, out of our sight. Then, reassured that all was well, we made our way from the marsh, and left the harriers to themselves for a couple of days while we went in search of other birds.

When we returned to our vigil at the harriers' nest, we found the chicks still in the original nest where we had put them. They were very lively, and were now covered in plentiful pure white down. They had large glamorous black eyes and pink mouths, and at this early age were delightful little creatures, without any savage tendencies. The hen soon returned to brood them, and as

Plate 62.—The hen Montagu's harrier shielding her young from the sun.

she settled down she tucked under her the remains of a young red-legged partridge that was lying on the nest, and brooded that too.

After about an hour the hen got up and stood on the side of the nest, seized the young partridge, and held it firmly on to the nest under her left talons. Then with a sharp upward twist she wrenched a piece off and swallowed it. More and more pieces were pulled off and swallowed until she came to some red meat devoid of feathers. This was offered in small pieces to the chicks, which all the time had kept up a continuous chorus of chirruping. All of them had a share, the meal lasting just over four minutes, and then the hen cleared up the remains herself, swallowing everything, including the legs.

It was just after this that we saw another food-pass. As before, the hen called at the approach of the cock, and kept up this high-pitched scream for about a minute while the cock circled overhead. Then, carefully disentangling herself from the chicks, she flew up to meet the cock and returned almost at once with a young pheasant.

The cock flew on and continued hunting across the marsh, and it was not long before we saw him return to the vicinity of the other nest and call that hen to take food from him. This made it appear that he was mated to both hens, and as on subsequent occasions we saw further evidence of his dual attachments, it is fairly safe to conclude that this was another case of polygamy.

The day was now turning warm with bright sunshine, and, as the hen brooded the chicks, she occasionally stood in a crouching attitude, spreading her wings and fanning her tail to make some shade for them. This was interesting to watch, especially as the youngsters wandered about and every now and then poked their heads out from under the hen; but suddenly in the midst of this we were treated to one of those exceptional incidents, the occurrence of which adds so much zest to bird-watching. The cock flew over, and, as usual, the hen called to him, her shrill note reminding us of the cry of the swift magnified many times in volume, when suddenly down he came to pay one of his rare visits to the nest. The hen was excited in his presence and stood quivering on the side of the nest, but his visit was very brief, and almost before we had time to take in the beauty of his pearly-grey plumage and striking yellow eye he was gone again, and the hen stood watching him depart.

The young harriers grew rapidly, and, as they grew, so they developed the typical predatory reactions. They pecked viciously at anything within reach and at each other, and whenever we attempted to touch them they rolled over on their backs and struck at us with their sharp little talons. As they began to feather, they were left on their own more and more while the hen was away hunting—a task which she was obliged to undertake, perhaps earlier than usual, as the cock began to give more attention to the other hen at the neighbouring nest.

We were unable to stay with these harriers throughout the whole of their fledging period, but we understand that they all survived to set out on their migrations, and, we hope, to continue the breed of this rather rare but delightful member of our British avifauna.

Plate 63.—The young harriers begin to show their feathers.

The Water-Rail

SOME BIRDS appear to have an uncanny sense of impending weather changes, and the water-rails we illustrate are a case in point. They had built their nest in shallow water on the fringe of a Broad in Norfolk at a point where the river is non-tidal. The nest was a substantial structure built amongst the growing sedge and on the reasonably firm foundation of the sedge roots. The cup stood some six inches above normal water level.

There were seven eggs when we found the nest, and incubation was well advanced. Everything seemed to be progressing normally when one day the water-rails began to work frantically to add to their nest structure. The cock took a share, and hurried to and fro collecting nesting material, while the hen sat on the eggs and pulled at such pieces of sedge as she could reach and arranged them, and the material that the cock had brought, around the rim of the nest. After a spell of this the hen got off the nest and began to collect material herself. Bringing as much as she could carry in her bill, she made several journeys and dropped her loads into the cup of the nest, till, satisfied with her efforts, she climbed back on to the nest and began to arrange her collection. We noticed that she shuffled and drew the fresh material under her in such a way that she forced it under the eggs and so raised them with the nest.

So intense was this activity that at one period we noted thirty-five visits by the cock bird in forty minutes. There was a noticeable demarcation line in the nest between the old material and the new, and, when finished, the nest was raised by some four inches above its original level.

We wondered at the cause for this sudden addition to the nest. Gradual additions are not uncommon, and many birds bring back pieces of nesting material whenever they return to the nest; but we had never before experienced the like of this behaviour by the water-rails. On the day in question the wind had swung to south-west, and the sky was threatening rain after a long spell of dry weather with north-easterly winds. Could this have influenced the birds? The rain held off for a further two days and no further building took place, but on the third day a little more work was done on the nest. That night the weather broke, and the level of the Broad rose considerably, so that, but for the recent additions, the nest of the water-rails must have been submerged.

Plate 64.—The water-rails built up their nest and escaped the flood.

The Heron

NOBODY can mistake the heron for any other British bird, for there is none other like it in appearance, habits or flight. True, some might call it a "crane," but though lacking in precision, the term would not be entirely wrong.

The heron occurs locally throughout the British Isles, in places where shallow waters provide it with good fishing grounds, for the bird lives largely on fish and other aquatic creatures, and catches them by standing or walking slowly in the shallows and seizing them with a quick jab of its powerful bill. It nests in colonies, somewhat like the rook, making a large nest of twigs in the tree-tops. The heronry is usually quite close to suitable feeding waters, and so, not unnaturally, we find the greatest concentrations of herons in East Anglia and South-East England, with considerable numbers also in Cheshire and Somerset.

The grey-backed, hunched-up form of the heron, standing motionless by the lakeside or the river's edge, is a not unfamiliar sight in many places, so it comes as rather a surprise to find that, according to a census taken by the British Trust for Ornithology in the ten years prior to the war, the heron population of England and Wales was no greater than about 4000 pairs, and was keeping remarkably steady at that figure. The explanation must, of course, be that the heron is so conspicuous on account of its size and characteristic pose and its unmistakable flight, that we see a large proportion of the birds that do exist.

The pictures that we reproduce were taken with the help of Mr. John Barlee in a comparatively large heronry in Cheshire. There were seventy-seven occupied nests, of which sixty-nine were in oak trees, two in willows, and the rest in alders and elms. All the trees in this particular wood were large, and the nests were, on the average, more than fifty feet high. It will be noticed from Plate 65 that the heron nests early. The oak had not yet burst into leaf, yet in a nearby nest there were young herons fully six weeks old. They must have hatched from eggs laid in the middle of February. There is, however, a good deal of variation, for another pair we saw in the same heronry were still building a nest in the third week of April.

Stately as it appears in flight, with the slow rhythmic beat of its huge wings, the heron is an awkward-looking bird as it alights in a tree. From the extremity of a bough it walks tight-rope fashion towards the nest, its long neck extended upwards to its full height. As the bird approaches the nest it usually calls loudly and harshly, and the chicks add to the noise by greeting the parent with a loud chattering. In respect of noise the heronry is like the rookery, and during the breeding-season there seems a continuous babel as first one nest and then another reaches a minor climax of activity.

[*Continued on page 102.*

Plate 65.—The heron alights on the tree tops.

Plate 66.—On guard by the side of the nest.

Feeding of the young is by regurgitation. In the very early stages the young seize the parent's bill, and after some tugging to and fro they take the regurgitated food direct from it. Later, a similar stimulation by the young causes the parent to disgorge the food on to the nest. As shown in Plate 69, the hen stands on a branch above and behind the nest. She bends her long legs, leans forwards and downwards, and stretches out her neck. The young all try to grab her bill, and an intermittent tug-of-war follows with violent wing-flapping. There is usually a scramble when the food is dropped on to the nest, especially if the young are at all hungry. In a typical case, one of the young quickly seized the food and turned his back on the others while he proceeded to swallow it. The other chicks fought hard and pecked at him furiously, so that he was nearly pushed over the edge of the nest; but the old bird took no notice and stood there, hunched up on the branch. A few minutes later the hen leaned forward again and began to retch, and the whole process was repeated, with more bill-tugging and fighting; and after a further interval the remaining chick was fed in like manner.

Hunting and feeding seem to make the heron's plumage into a very soiled condition, and she spends a considerable time in preening herself. Like her near relative the bittern, the heron has patches of powder-down on the breast and she makes use of the powder to clean her feathers, transferring it with her bill and rubbing it into the feathers as she preens.

One of the most surprising things about a heronry is the way it withstands strong winds in spite of its apparent susceptibility. A fresh breeze seems to

[*Continued on page 107.*

Plate 67.—The heron at home.

Plate 68.—Preparing to feed the young.

Plate 69.—The meal in progress.

Plate 70.—The heron takes off.

Plate 71.—Flying over the heronry.

change the whole conditions in the tree-tops, as we have found to our discomfort in various tree-top hides, and the herons soon appear to be in difficulties in a rising wind. Young and old are in danger of being blown off the nests, and some of the young ones do in fact succumb, but the great majority must obviously survive this danger, or the heronries would not persist, as many have done, for generations and even for centuries.

Plate 72.—The Slavonian grebe.

The Slavonian Grebe

WHAT a thrill there is in coming for the first time on something rare, especially if it is at the same time a thing of beauty. The Slavonian grebe is both, and we were delighted to have the opportunity of watching a pair in one of their breeding haunts in a Scottish loch. It was the early part of June, and the summer sunshine was bringing out the full glory of the landscape colours as we made our way to the nest; and then, as we approached the reed-fringed loch, the sight that met our eyes was one long to be remembered. The water reflected the azure of a clear sky, and the green and brown reeds growing in the shallows cast their trembling reflections on the rippled surface.

We drew near and saw the nest, a mound of half-decayed vegetation some fifteen inches across and protruding a few inches above the surface of the water. It was well sheltered by the growing reed and appeared to be on a firm foundation. In many respects it looked like the nest of a dabchick, but we soon knew its real owner, for the cock Slavonian grebe came boldly into the picture.

He was a fine bird in his colourful breeding plumage. As he paddled easily along on the calm surface of the water, his chestnut breast and neck were much in evidence. From time to time he turned his rich black head, revealing the striking golden-orange plumes which, from a point just behind the eye, project backwards and upwards slightly beyond the back of his head and give him a very distinguished appearance.

We noticed at once that this bird was much less shy than the great crested grebes we had watched, and we understand that this is a characteristic of the species. The Slavonian grebe does not dive at once at the approach of an intruder, as does his larger relative; and often when disturbed he does not dive at all, but takes to flight, skimming for some distance across the water before becoming fully airborne.

This grebe had three eggs when we first saw the nest, but two of these disappeared during the next few days, and we feared that some nearby black-headed gulls must be raiding the nest and that they might cause the grebes to desert it. Happily this was not the case, and the grebes continued to tend the one remaining egg. Brooding was only intermittent at this stage, and it seemed that incubation proper, which usually begins when the clutch is complete, had not yet begun.

A considerable amount of time was spent in swimming about in the vicinity of the nest, pulling at half-decayed and submerged weed, and bringing it to the nest to build up the structure. Such addition to the nest is a common feature throughout the nesting period with many aquatic birds, and particularly where

[*Continued on page 114.*

Plates 73 and 74.—The cock displays his golden-yellow tufts as he bows his head in front of the hen. He then swims round the nest, shaking his head from side to side.

Plate 75.—The cock hesitated when behind the hen.

Plate 76.– The cock Slavonian grebe displaying on the nest.

Plate 77.—After raising his head he lowers it nearly to the water level.

the nests are built in the water it is often necessary to make up for wastage and preserve the structure from disintegration.

During this business of nest-repair there were, from time to time, interesting courtship displays between the cock and hen grebes. They varied somewhat in their general pattern, but always there was a spectacular spreading of the golden ear-tufts and an excited calling between the two birds. On one occasion the hen had been brooding the single egg for a short while when she suddenly began to call. Almost at once the cock appeared from out of the reeds and swam towards the nest. Both birds became very excited. The hen leaned forward, stretched out her neck, and curved it downwards with a snake-like motion till her chin was almost resting on the water. The cock swam quickly round the nest, swaying his head from side to side, and up and down, to display the full splendour of his vivid ear-tufts to his mate. Coming then directly in front of the hen, he stopped and turned towards her, and lowering his head till his bill nearly touched the water, he presented his velvety black crown surmounted by the two golden plumes in a final salute of exceptional beauty. He remained thus for some moments, while the hen, lying prostrate, seemed to stare at him, as though hypnotised. His next action was to circle the nest again, and then coming round behind the hen, he paused. He paddled backwards a little away from the nest, and then, swimming rapidly forwards, he leapt out of the water and on to the hen's back, and, with his large white lobed feet, smacked her shoulders alternately in rapid succession before coition took place. The hen remained quite passive during the proceedings until after the cock had left, when she did a little preening to her feathers and then resumed normal brooding.

The following day there was renewed vigorous nest repair interspersed with further nuptials, and an interesting variant on this occasion was that, subsequent to a display like that just described, the birds changed over duties at the nest and the cock took a spell of brooding. He was somewhat restless, and from time to time got off the nest to go and fetch more weed. Back on the nest again he began to call, and spread his plumes in display. This time his head was not lowered to the water, but his neck was stretched up at an angle of about forty-five degrees. The hen arrived and swam about in the vicinity. She busied herself collecting weed, and appeared to take no notice of her mate's performance. He watched every movement she made, and presently tried leaning forward with his neck depressed towards her, but she would have none of it and eventually swam away into the reeds, where he followed a few minutes later.

Fascinating as it had been, the display of these birds was not the only interesting event we were to see at this nest. Two days after the incidents just recorded, we noticed another egg had arrived in the nest, and it was followed by a third, and a fourth. The one egg remaining from the first clutch had thus held the birds to this nest, and they had rebuilt, and laid another clutch, on

[*Continued on page 117.*

Plate 78.—Some of the grebes display attitudes are peculiarly grotesque.

Plate 79.—The cock, standing on the side of the nest, prepares to brood the eggs.

the foundations of their first attempt. The various phases of the breeding cycle were thus curiously mixed up. Courtship and display, nest-building, and even spasmodic brooding, had all gone on at the same time, and it was only after the beginning of the second clutch of eggs that events began to settle into their normal cycle. The displays ceased, more regular brooding became the order of the day, and, when the eggs were left, they were covered with weed as is the usual custom among the birds of this family. Unfortunately we were not able to stay long enough in the district to see the Slavonian grebe family hatch out, but we shall not forget the fascinating experience that they did afford us while we were with them.

The Wigeon

ALTHOUGH the wigeon nests regularly in the northern part of Scotland and a few pairs nest from time to time in other parts of the British Isles, it is as a winter visitor that we best know this bird. Its normal breeding range extends across Eastern and Northern Europe and includes Iceland, and from these haunts the wigeon comes in its thousands to spend the winter months in our islands and around our shores.

From about mid-September to March the wigeon is a familiar sight on many inland waters, but it is on tidal estuaries and mud-flats that we find it in the greatest numbers, for it has a marked preference for salt water, and feeds largely on a sea-grass called *Zostera* that grows abundantly on many muddy stretches around our coasts.

Where its feeding-grounds are comparatively undisturbed, the wigeon may be seen feeding by day and making the most of its opportunities while the tide is low, but it is a shy bird, and in many places remains swimming about off-shore by day and only flies in to feed at dusk.

As he wades about in the shallows, the drake is readily recognised by his dark chestnut head surmounted by a creamy yellow forehead and crown, and by a prominent white patch on his greyish wings. When seen at close quarters he is remarkably beautiful, with a pinkish flush on his breast, and finely-grained markings on his grey body and wings. As is usual in the duck family, his mate is much duller in plumage, her upper parts being chiefly a warm brown with dark speckles; a coloration that makes her comparatively inconspicuous when she is sitting.

The nest is usually on moorland or on rough, tussocky pasture, and is made of heather twigs, bracken stems and grass, and is plentifully lined with down and feathers. In these islands the seven or eight creamy-coloured eggs are seldom laid before the middle of May, and it was in fact well into June when we secured our photograph of the hen by the nest. Incubation takes about three and a half weeks and then, at a very early age, the ducklings are led by the duck to the nearest water, and are tended and guarded there until they can fend for themselves.

Plate 80.—Wigeon at nest.

The Teal

THE smallest of our ducks, and, with the exception of the mallard, one of the most widely distributed, the teal is readily recognised both in the air and on the ground or water. Apart from its size, it is distinguished by a characteristic rapid flight, its swerving and darting action being rather similar to that of the redshank; and in winter, when the teal gather into flocks of considerable size, it is notable for the way the birds keep together, wheeling and diving in perfect unison as if at word of command.

The teal breeds in most parts of the British Isles, though in only limited numbers in the south, and is fairly catholic in its choice of habitat. Damp moorland and swampy heath is perhaps its favourite haunt, but the nest may be on dry ground among heather, gorse or bracken. It is almost invariably on the ground and is well sheltered, making it somewhat difficult to locate. The nest-lining usually includes dead leaves, but it is the downy feathers in the lining which serve as a useful guide to the identity of the owner. A description in words cannot satisfactorily replace practical guidance on this point, but it is of interest to note that the down in the teal's nest is small and rather dark in colour, and lacks the striking white edges exhibited by the down of the garganey, with which alone it might otherwise be confused.

Unlike the wigeon, the teal favours fresh water rather than salt, and the majority of birds winter on lakes, reservoirs and sewage farms, though considerable numbers do resort to the coast and to tidal mud-flats, especially during severe weather. Those birds which breed in this country tend to stay here for the winter, but the flocks are very largely swelled by winter visitors from Iceland and the lands around the Baltic.

Plate 81.—The teal is the smallest of our ducks.

The Mallard

THERE IS something fascinating in the sight of a pair of wild duck flying swiftly across the evening sky. The rapid wing-beats and the head stretched well forward of the wings give an impression of urgency to their mission, and we inevitably linger to watch their progress. If we are near them, and the light is good enough, we may see sufficient detail to identify them with certainty, but the novice must be cautious, for there are no less than nineteen different species of wild duck to be seen regularly in the British Isles, and fourteen of these are resident throughout the year and stay to breed in varying numbers. Some of these are restricted to certain localities, but the mallard is very widely distributed, and is to be found almost anywhere where a pond or other stretch of water provides the aquatic exercise and feeding facilities that the birds like.

The mallard is not particular about the choice of a nesting-site, but usually builds in fairly thick cover under a bush or hedge. It may occasionally use an open hollow tree or the cup of a pollarded willow in which to lay its eggs, but the site will almost certainly be near water, as the duck normally leads her offspring to the water for safety soon after they are hatched. The nest is usually lined with grass and dead leaves, together with down and feathers, the latter being peculiarly characteristic and readily identified by the double dark patch that occurs towards the tip.

Like many of the duck family the drake mallard takes very little hand in the rearing of the young. He is most attentive to his mate up to the beginning of incubation, and jealously drives off any other drake that may intrude, but while the duck is sitting he goes off and joins company with other drakes similarly situated, and they stay together in a flock, often on some nearby secluded water. His absence is in some respects a safety measure, for his bright colouring displayed near the nest might attract the attention of passing predators, but he obviously keeps in touch with the duck, for he sometimes visits his family after the eggs have hatched, and he certainly rejoins his mate at a later date, for mallards are normally to be seen in pairs even during the winter, and it is thought that they pair for life.

Plate 82.—The mallard.

The Partridge

ALTHOUGH man's study of birds in general dates only from comparatively recent times, his interest in game-birds goes back into the remote past. The partridge was certainly recognised as a valuable table bird before the Norman Conquest, and its preservation by landowners has been customary for many centuries.

Even without artificial rearing, the partridge is well established as a breeding species in most parts of England and Wales. It is particularly plentiful in the south and east, inhabiting especially those tracts of country where rough pasture and heathland with gorse and other cover is interspersed with agricultural land, for here the partridge finds shelter for her nest and food for her family.

The compact form of the partridge, its round body, short tail, and small head—beautifully flecked in reddish-brown—are too well known to need much description, but the behaviour and habits of the bird in its wild state are not so familiar. We have had the good fortune to watch several pairs of partridges during the breeding season, and, especially after watching the ducks, we have been impressed by the loyalty and devotion of the cock partridge to his mate.

Whereas in most of the duck family it is usual for the drakes to take no part in the affairs at the nest, the cock partridge is a most faithful husband. He takes no part in the actual incubation of the eggs, but in most cases that we have seen he comes periodically to escort his mate to feed and brings her back to the nest afterwards, walking stealthily through the undergrowth to avoid attracting any attention to the nest.

At the time of hatching, the cock partridge is an eager and helpful attendant on the hen. He sits near the nest, and as the first few chicks hatch out and become dry, he encourages them to struggle over to shelter under him while they gain strength for their further journeyings. This assistance is particularly valuable in assuring the safe development of the family, for the partridge normally has as many as twelve to sixteen eggs, and the brood of chicks would be more than the hen alone could manage, especially as they usually all hatch out within two or three hours.

Soon after the last chick is hatched, the cock and hen entice the young ones away from the nest and into fresh cover. They grow rapidly, and can fly when little more than a fortnight old, but, presumably for their own protection, the covey keeps together right through the summer, autumn, and winter, and only disperses with the approach of the next breeding season.

Plate 83.—The haunt of the partridge.

The Pheasant

Just as in *Birds of the Day*, we concluded with a semi-domesticated bird, the swan, so in the present volume we choose the pheasant; and what finer tail-piece could there be?

The gaudy plumage of the cock pheasant, his green head with bright-red wattles, his chestnut back and wings variously flecked with black, buff, and reddish-purple, and his long, tapering tail boldly barred with black and edged with copper, are indications of his exotic ancestry. The pheasant is not really a native of this country, but was brought here by the Romans from a race that is indigenous in the region around the Black Sea. From time to time other importations were made, particularly of Chinese birds, so that the pheasant as we know it to-day is of mixed descent, and considerable variations of plumage are found between one bird and another.

As might be expected of so large a bird, the pheasant spends a great part of its time on the ground, but it flies up to the shelter of trees when disturbed, and normally roosts in trees. The flight is rapid and direct, the short wings whirring noisily as the bird rises; but its aerial excursions are short as a rule, and when sufficient height has been gained the bird glides silently and drops down into cover a little way off.

It is problematical how long the pheasant would survive in this country if it were not artificially reared and protected. Many birds do breed in the wild state, and, because they have such a very varied diet of animal and vegetable matter, they have little difficulty in getting sufficient for their existence; but the vast majority are hatched out under domestic hens as foster-mothers, and they are fed by their keepers and encouraged by the suppression of their natural enemies—the rat, the stoat, and the fox.

The pheasant is to be found in most parts of the British Isles, though it seems that there are only small numbers of really wild birds in Ireland. It likes plenty of cover, such as that afforded by brambles and other undergrowth in a fairly thick wood, but it likes to have available as well some open country, such as parkland, pasture and cultivation. The nest is usually on the ground in the shelter of a hedgerow or a copse, and it is often cleverly concealed under brambles, grass or other herbage. With this protection and the natural protective coloration of the hen pheasant, the nest may easily be unnoticed by the casual passer-by.

There is no doubt that, apart from his value as a game bird, the pheasant is an attractive member of our avifauna, and though he cannot perhaps be classed as an ally of the farmer, he is not without his points as a devourer of insect pests. Certainly our woods in spring would be the poorer without his resounding call.

Plate 84.—The pheasant and chick.